To Bloom in the Shadows

Jazmine Thompson

BookLeaf Publishing

Presentation by *BookLeaf Publishing*

Web: www.bookleafpub.com

E-mail: info@bookleafpub.com

ISBN: 9789357211062

First edition 2022

DEDICATION

This is a labor of love for my mother, the girl who tried. Although she stumbled, and felt the shame that came with that embedded in her soul, she continued to try. May we all have the guts to keep trying despite all obstacles. May we all have the guts to continue living.

May my mother rest knowing, that her memory will be immortalized by her daughter...her legacy lives on. I think of the song, "Savage Daughter" by Wyndreth Berginsdottir;

"I am my mothers savage daughter!

The one who runs barefoot cursing sharp stones

I am my mothers savage daughter!

I will not cut my hair, I will not lower my voice!"

And I am.

1.

I am art
A broken mosaic of unfinished "would-be" masterpieces
A collection of scattered should be's and deafening what ifs
Is it wrong to call myself art if my canvas is still blank?
I am the yet to be discovered 8th wonder of the world
If only I could silence the voices in my head screaming at me to put down the pen
If only I could listen better to the whispers of the broken glass at my feet
I am as untouched as the sky after a tornado
The earth ripped and frayed from the storm I unleashed
I am a muse that gave her magic to a man from a kingdom of dust, where nothing grows
I am scorched earth surrounded by babbling brooks
Fail me and I will destroy you
Feed me and I will grow for you
I am tempered glass, stained by the blood I've shed at my own hand

I am a hundred unwritten sonnets, waiting to come to life at the hands of a man who does not know love
The light at the end of the tunnel is me, I can taste it
But I fear my train is barreling down the wrong track
I am art, you see
Because art is tragedy and wasted opportunity

what's self love got to do with it?

I see the words of other poets
And realize I'll fall short
My words will never be as eloquent
I'll never have such depth
I'll never be able to move a stone cold heart to tears
Never see their expression warm by my words
But is this just fear taking the lead?
and what if...what if I don't let it beat me?

what if I believed in me? wouldn't that be a sight to see...

backup plans and explosions

I wish I could go back in time and tell the girl that was so wrapped up in Moulin Rouge that one day someone would look at her, sing “your song” to her and mean it. I wish I could go back and tell her she didn’t have to settle for crumbs and call it love. She deserved the whole damn dinner and a show.

gordita.

My fat has not kept me safe.
That's a myth.
It has never stopped grown men from staring
And carrying on about what they'd like to see me wearing
Ushered into dark rooms and cornered
Afraid to say no, afraid of being labeled undesirable
A secret passion by moonlight, a denial by morning
My body holds the memory of every man and woman who has used her as a lifeboat while she was drowning
I don't want to keep talking
....why am I still talking?
Do I even deserve to have a voice after all those years of silence?
And half smiles
The countless showers that burned my skin
Trying to peel away who was just let in
How am I supposed to know what intimacy is
When the first person to show me the way forced their way in
My fat did not keep me safe
That's a myth

It never stopped the pleading and guilt trips and the wearing down of my “no” until I gave up a piece of me
So this self love is a little hard, you see?
I haven’t learned how to make my “no” guilt free
I haven’t learned how to love my body in its entirety
I’m trying, I promise, to forgive a younger me
For not knowing that sex and intimacy were to be shared, not taken
That my love was to be deep rooted and stirred within me, not shaken

why did i give up so much of me for you?

Sunsets used to bring a promise of adventure but
now they're just a reminder
A small goodbye as the sun sleeps
it's almost as if I can feel us dying
I see the memory in the present and that's not
really living in the moment is it?
So…how do I get back to loving the moon when
even she hides...
when she ushers in the end...

I'm lost and I can't find my way back home.

i hold onto the ghosts of my past because i loved them enough for the both of us and still... i couldn't make them stay

Do you see me up here?
I'm trying to be seen.
Because if you see me then I can begin to be freed.
I stare hopelessly out of this window, anxiously waiting for a glimpse of your face
I fear I can only love from afar
I feel trapped in this place
I live in this fragile tall house, unaware of the language
Praying you see me in all of my unrequited anguish
Is love an antique?
like this tall house I confined myself in?
or is it like your world?
enchanting and inviting...
I hope one day you'll see me and we could leave together
until then you hold the key

I'll love you from this window forever...

2021.

Death is a cruel friend
Or is it life that I can't comprehend?
You could be here one minute and then gone forever
Life really is as fragile as a feather
Knocked around by the wind, unbalanced and untethered.
Tethered…
…we were tethered
Now even that is severed
How am I only 29 and buried both of my mothers?
How can I prepare my children for their own befores and afters
When my own heart feels like the destruction after a series of tornados

0 to 2020

It was supposed to be a taser
A forgotten turn signal
A car air freshener
A traffic stop
A walk home
A stop for snacks
A restful nights sleep
A grocery run
Mundane actions became preludes to funerals
There's blood on their hands, our streets, our air
Don't walk that way, don't talk that way
Comply just to survive....please survive
They can't breathe....I can't breathe.
He called out "momma please"
People at home just turning the channel on the tv
Rocking themselves to sleep, "it's been so long since slavery"
Victims on trial, their murderers go free
We're still just strange fruit hanging on their tree
They owe Billie an apology

a love letter to myself.

you were named after a flower that blooms in
winter
after a princess that leaves the comfort of her
palace in search of connection
but you feel that beyond your self-imposed cage
there is no ground to walk on
only quicksand at your feet
J a z m i n e
you were named after a flower that blooms when
others die
yet you run from the power within
you believe you are nobody
when you are an infinite marvel of this Universe
creation runs through your veins like the very
blood that keeps you alive
don't go off somewhere else searching for a
traveler to call home
you belong in your own garden, in your own
palace
don't go off somewhere else when the only home
you've ever needed was right within your grasp,
within the garden in your heart

shame

I speak for the dreamers, the ones born from nightmares
I speak for the large eyes staring at the moon, marveling at her freedom to change
I speak for the silent voices, waiting for a chance to be heard.
and although my voice trembles, words burning like acid in my throat
I speak for the ones who thrive in the underworld, unable to be themselves above
I speak for the child in me who couldn't
I speak for my mom who knew the touch of a man too early, too roughly
I speak for the little girl in her that needed acceptance and never found it
until she reached the moon, the stars, the space in between
I understand now why the moon hides herself in darkness
some secrets are too catastrophic to be shone in the light

i owe myself.

I am a writer who has lost her spark
A lover whose has caged her heart
A starving artist without the art
The emptiness and pain lives and mutates
I find myself lost in the works of Larson and Poe
Van Gogh and Miranda
Only one of them has seen the fruits of his labor
Am I to follow the footsteps of none?
Drowned in my own unused potential
Why is it that I believe in everyone else more
than I believe in me?
This is a curse to feel this deeply
To see the world as I see it…
And yet…
I allow the implosion of words to destroy me,
body and soul
What if I only ever talk about my dreams?
What if they turn sour within me?
Maybe I'm scared…
Maybe the problem is that I want my art to
prove my worth
To show all those who threw me aside that they
were wrong
Maybe the problem is that my art just wants
to…breathe

And I have given it an impossible task…
I treat my art like they treated me…
But when will I finally see
All I need is a pen and a diary…
To make my vision a reality
Let it be imperfect, let it spill out of me
It's time to make me proud of me

Adele, how do you deal with self doubt?

I drink wine, too
But I don't know if I could've put it in the same
way as you
I'm afraid I have the wrong to catch lightning
with
Its uncanny, unsettling, and totally insane
...how well you've untangled the quiet stages of
my life
I wonder how the same stars that aligned for you
seemed to miss me so catastrophically
I have so much inside of me, bursting to reach
creation
Why do I stop me from creating?
If I step off the ledge and let myself breathe the
same air as every artist before me
Will I fall?
Will I fail?
Will I stay on this mountaintop and never leap?
Becoming one with dirt and shame
And then be forgotten all the same?
Or will my worlds and words never see
daylight?
Will I never be free?
Even now, knowing that I'm the key...

I wanna believe that the same stars that aligned
for them
Also aligned for me, maybe?

shadow work

Death and I have a special love affair
We dance, I let go
We meet, he lets go
And sometimes, when the moon is full
I am ensnared in his passion and warmth
and it's not a sure thing that I'll escape his embrace
And some nights, I don't want to find my way back to morning
but his scent lingers longer than he does
even Death wants me as a friend instead of a longtime lover
and yet, I'll always wait for his whispers
I'm faithful to his shadows
Death doesn't keep score but I do…

fire and brimstone..

Is loving me like dying?
Because if it is,
If it feels like destruction and fire
I would treat me like a pariah, too
I know I have tasted true love…
I know I have held it in my hands and…
And I know that the minute I breathe it in, it
falls through my grasp like quicksand
I just know I'm tired of falling asleep with roses
in my hands
Only for them to be dead by morning
And me, alone again, the sun shining through
the window, in mourning

grief

Here's what they don't tell you about growing up:

That night you spent crying an ocean of tears…ends
You'll curse the sun in the morning through bloodshot eyes
And loneliness will creep in through the blinds
But the world will continue to turn
And you, well you'll learn what it means to yearn
No one tells you about the days you'll be begging to feel real
So you search for substance
But the kind you find suffocates you
They don't tell you that what numbs you kills you quick
And what feels safe is actually a mirage

They don't tell you that the earth will have gone around the sun a million times
And you'll still feel like the wounded one crying an ocean of tears
On that one endless night

GRAY

I stood in front of everyone who has
misunderstood me
and apologized for existing
thanked them for still caring
as if I wasn't worthy of love and affection and a
happy ending

it will be the last time I ever say "I'm sorry for
existing"
I don't owe anymore apologies for bleeding
while I was wounded

reborn, renewed, reset

I will not spend the rest of my life recovering
from people who did not love me
apologizing for the way my actions screamed
"help me!"
I always told myself if I could've turned back the
hands of time, I would've done things differently
but that was then...
I no longer cringe being told I'm strong
I no longer wish to desperately belong
I've given up the self hatred that stuck to my
bones like molasses
I am not a broken poster child for the masses
THIS is my declaration
call it, a deep reclamation
I no longer live in the empty caves where
darkness and memories collide and coexist
I reached the sun
but unlike Icarus, I can not be burned
I am like my sisters and mothers before me, a
Phoenix, unbound and flying by Divine
intervention
My ancestors rejoice as their prayers have been
answered
I settle my gaze only on our shared Ascension

o x y t o c i n d u m p

I don't understand why life doesn't stop the
moment a soul leaves
a moment of reprieve, slow down time to release
a lifetime of love and grief
imagine if we could all take a year or two
to mourn the loss of love departed
to celebrate, to laugh, to cry,
to scream into the void
to say goodbye
and only when we're ready does our day restart
and we can keep going without such a
carnivorous wound festering in our heart

legacy

I've lost your shirt
I've lost your rice pot
I've lost the vivid memory of your laughter
I have to strain to remember the way your hands
felt, always ice cold
but what I haven't lost is the sense that you were
here
you're not in history books
you weren't an innovator of global proportions
but you were here
You were the entire universe to two little girls
questioning their right to exist
Sometimes I question if I once knew so much
love and I question most things but you were
here...you were real.
You were more than your bible, more than your
crossword puzzles
You were far beyond your tough, your mean,
your anger
You were the first Phoenix, ablaze by your own
resilience
you were the entire galaxy to two little girls
waging war on themselves
you made the pain of existing worth it
and I pray you felt it

God, I hope you felt it.

you're the only real thing i know

We had a lavendar plant in a pot that tipped over
Life got busy and we forgot to put it back into
it's pot
the lavendar decided to hell with us
and grew until her roots were firmly back in the
earth.

-the only real thing I know about life, death, and
love.

3.

I heard the most beautiful voice coming from the woods
She sang a song so sweet
Captivating and Mesmerizing
I searched for her voice
Needing to see the creature who sang so wonderfully
I crept through the woods following the call
And there she sat, dressed in white
Her long dress draped around her
Her hair moving in the breeze
She lifted her face and I couldn't believe my eyes
She wasn't a stranger, she was... me

And in my head I heard a soft voice
"Welcome home"

www.ingramcontent.com/pod-product-compliance
Lightning Source LLC
Chambersburg PA
CBHW051759130826
49812CB00033B/1204
9789357211062